Bedtime Meditations for Kids

Discover the Ultimate Guide to Achieve Mindfulness to Make Your Children Fall Asleep Fast. Help Your Child Calm Down and Relax Listening to Amazing Fables.

Megan Miller

ISBN: 978-1-914358-18-0

The information provided herein is stated to be truthful and consistent, in that any liability, in terms of inattention or otherwise, by any usage or abuse of any policies, processes, or directions contained within is the solitary and utter responsibility of the recipient reader. Under no circumstances will any legal responsibility or blame be held against the publisher for any reparation, damages, or monetary loss due to the information herein, either directly or indirectly.

Respective authors own all copyrights not held by the publisher.

The information herein is offered for informational purposes solely, and is universal as so. The presentation of the information is without contract or any type of guarantee assurance.

The trademarks that are used are without any consent, and the publication of the trademark is without permission or backing by the trademark owner. All trademarks and brands within this book are for clarifying purposes only and are owned by the owners themselves, not affiliated with this document.

Table of Contents

Introduction

Bedtime stories are considered to foster connections between parent and infant, and to prepare children for sleep. But, lately, researchers have introduced other powers to this nocturnal activity. They tell, when you and your little one sail to the Wild Stuff Land with Max, or eat green eggs with Sam, you are literally improving your child's brain growth. Neural work indicates that while parents and guardians interact orally with babies, who include reading children to them, they learn much better than we ever thought imaginable, "says G. Reid Lyon, Ph.D., Head of Child Growth and Behavior Division at Bethesda's National Institute of Child Safety and Human Development, MD.

Production Of An Inner Dictionary

To better improve an infant's language abilities, parents can use storytime as a contact starting point, says Lise Eliot, Ph.D., assistant professor of psychology at Chicago Medical School and author of What's Going on up There? Why the mind and brain develop during the First Five Years of Life. For example, if a mother refers to the baseball cap of Curious George and asks her son, "Do you have a hat like that?" she gives him the chance to use words properly.

Nevertheless, Dr. Eliot cautions parents not to fix speech abnormalities of their child on a daily basis. "My own kid still assumes he is, as she says in 'That's the hat for him.'" So I'm not thinking 'no, you'll know his cap,' because I don't want to dissuade him. Then I clearly model the right speech by accurately repeating his sentence: 'Indeed! This is his cap! "Reading for a kid in time can broaden the vocabulary much further than simply talking to her. That's how books introduce children to ideas and things like porridge or kangaroos that are not part of their daily interaction.

A Little More

This word is used as a simple effort on a child's part to delay bedtime. Yet what kids and parents do not know is that reading a book daily can help a child develop his / her thinking skills. They don't recall it all the first time kids read a book, says Virginia Walter, Ph.D., an associate professor at the California University, Los Angeles 'graduate school of education and communications sciences. However when they hear it over and over again, they continue to recognize trends and loops, realizing that if one page says, "Brown bear, brown bear, what you see?" the next page will know the brown bear's reaction: "I see a red bird looking at me." They will even start to anticipate what will happen next based on their past knowledge ("Ah, no, the wolf is going to blow down the house!"). Afterward, in other areas, from math and science to music and literature, these experiences in pattern identification, series interpretation, and outcome predicting can help students. But reading aloud doesn't have to end before kids can read alone; indeed, that is when they develop reading comprehension skills, Dr. Walter notes.

Ask a kid to experiment what she thinks will happen next, or if she would finish a tale otherwise.

Also in puberty, researchers suggest parents maintain the practice. By choosing books that are only above a teen's skill point, you can continue to expose her to new vocabulary

and expand her repertoire. In addition, reading aloud will provide a platform for interacting with babies. "It's much easier to think about a complicated issue in the framework of your personal life," Dr. Walter says. "When the question occurs in personal life then you might say, 'Remember what we've been thinking about?'" She suggests reading Terabithia's iconic Katherine Patterson Bridge for communicating to adolescents regarding death; likewise, the Little House on the Prairie series offer families the opportunity to address stereotypes.

Pleasant Snuggles

To further enjoy the developmental benefits of reading, it would be enjoyable to visit a kid with books, says Peter Gorski, M.D., chairman of the Early Childhood Committee of the American Academy of Pediatrics. "You want him, above all, to associate reading with mental warmth and enjoyment," he says.

If kids feel comfortable and safe they will also decrease their anxiety while reading aloud. When a child undergoes pressure such as bullying or beginning a new school his brain attempts to protect him by releasing the hormone cortisol that activates the body's response of "fight or flight." In fact, cortisol can help children endure regular stress in small doses. However in greater numbers it may obstruct knowledge.

While no scientific studies have been performed about how bedtime books impact children with elevated rates of cortisol, neuroscientists agree it is reasonable that reading a common book would calm a child when snuggling next to a mom, thereby that the levels of cortisol to make him concentrate

more. Cuddle up in a cozy place with your boy, his favorite toys and nearby stuffed animals to strengthen the calming nature of the story time at home.

"Relax and just have fun with your kid," Dr. Gorski says. "Imagine what the romantic time you spend interacting with your own cortisol rates is going to do!"

They particularly love hearing a story from their mum or father just before bedtime. Reading bedtime stories for children is a perfect way to connect with them, and fosters a love of reading. Reading to children makes them love books and become writers on their own. It even sharps memory, strengthens language and encourages creative thinking.

The bedtime tale is the best way to finish the infant's day and put them into a beautiful restful sleep. Over hundreds of years the interpretation of the bedtime story over children has been included. The bedtime tale is a daily storytelling practice and is handed on from generation to generation. Classical bedtime tales like Cinderella, Rapunzel and the Velveteen Rabbit have been repeated from adult to infant to grandchild, conveying collective experiences of happy times in a fairy tale

Chapter 1: A Definitive Guide of Meditation

Meditation is not about becoming another person, a different individual or just a better human. It's about being open to experience, and getting a clear sense of perspective. You're not going to close down your thoughts or feelings. You are able to look at them without bias. So then, you will make them properly understood. To make things even more concrete, we felt the perfect way to do it was as follows. After reading hundreds of definitions we found that there were some sections in general in both meanings. Those are:

• Soul relaxing

• A main area of concentration

• Emptying and purifying the soul

In brief, meditation can be summarized as follows: "Meditation is a calming activity that helps you to turn your total, unbiased mind on the present moment" Meditation is not about becoming another person, different individual or great. This is about sharpening one's perspective and having a clear perception and appreciation of one's own culture.

Meditation is a practice that is becoming much more popular worldwide. Madonna, Hugh Jackman, Katy Perry and Clint Eastwood are only a couple of instances of celebrities who meditate regularly. However, meditation was used often up to Hollywood. The archeologists find drawings from 3000-5500 B.C. This demonstrates a meditating man.

So what is this mystical thing that has encircled mankind for millennia? In fact, it is not simple to understand what meditation is in words, because to realize it truly, you have to practice meditation and experience it in your own body.

1.1 Forums of Meditation

There are so many ways of therapy, all of which differ in the manner you practice it and its aims.

There are a thousand forms out there and opportunities to know how to meditate, to tell the truth. While advanced training is needed for some forms of mediation methods, most are open to anyone.

For the same types of treatment, you'll pass across various networks with separate names. But in fact, don't be too clear. Ultimately, it's just crucial that you consider the different forms of meditating, and that you practice the meditation appropriately, and benefit from the results.

Here we speak about certain essential ways of Meditation;

1.2 Meditation Perception

Consciousness meditation aims to sharpen perception and achieve a state of mindfulness. Mindfulness is a condition where you relax on dwelling on all that is occurring at the moment. You notice something unfolding around you without any understanding, decision or comparison. Careful therapy has been shown to reduce fear, insomnia, tiredness, discomfort and sickness. This is extremely simple and everyone can do it everywhere. For certain schools, children are taught mindfulness as it is so simple and helps improve concentration, perception, memory and mental self-control.

This method is the best way for students to meditate and a wonderful chance to move into the mediation area because it is really simple to use and also has a good impact on attitude. You'll see the first improvements in one single counseling session.

To some it will be their mode of go-to meditation in mindfulness. Particularly this approach has little spiritual meaning and is oriented to the physical and mental benefits. Meditation should be carried out with care, with the eyes open or closed.

1.3 Meditation of Vipassana

We originally chose not to attach any faith or metaphysical meditations to this list, but Vipassana meditation currently belongs to the country's most important modes of meditation.

Vipassana meditation is the most popular form of Buddhist meditation. The purpose is ultimately to provide insights into the essence and significance of life to the mediator.

After years of practice, the Mediators seem to understand the meaning of reality and existence. And you can only learn those findings after years of dedication. There are virtually no short term benefits for Vipassana.

Mediators may note shifts in concentration, stress and motivation after only a few months. Nevertheless, the deepest metaphysical insights occur only after a few years. Through mediation session shall last for a total of an hour. Setting an alarm clock is best, and when meditating you don't spend too much time dreaming. Vipassana therapy aids in the physical, mental, and moral context. Your emphasis and devotion would not only enhance but also reinforce the spiritual connection.

1.4 Conclusive Meditation

Conclusive meditation, or focused meditation, is a relaxing method in which you focus all of the attention on a particular topic during the mediation session. That subject may be a physical item (couch, chair, and table), your being, part of your anatomy, objects surrounding you, or something in your imagination that you can visualize.

The most important aspect you need to hold in mind in this type of meditation is that you must continually switch your focus back to the specific subject while your eyes begin to wander. Let the expectations evolve, without trying to change them. Just note, to let go of them.

Place emphasis on the subject you want to respond to. Most people choose their own water. Don't try to push the emphasis on the target, and don't be frustrated if you get overwhelmed or start having problems. It just creates anxiety, and a sense of intimidation. If you feel too distracted, just concentrate on what's hot.

When selecting the subject for the concentrated meditation, ensure that the subject evokes pleasant feelings without creating too much excitement or irritation. When choosing an object that's important to you, make sure your memories don't get disturbed. The goal should be to concentrate on the entity itself, not on the objects you are connected to.

Pay as little heed as possible to such distracting feelings. The aim of concentrative meditation is to prepare the mind for continued focus. If thoughts or feelings come to your mind, perceive them no matter what type of stuff, and then put back your focus to the study stage.

But you completely shouldn't ignore certain emotions and opinions. Only because it's not feasible which causes you to feel sad, frustrated or irritated, this distracts you even more.

This needs quite a lot of work to hold the attention centered. When you concentrate too hard on the goal and neglect everything around you, you may feel overwhelmed and slow down your spiritual development. If you focus too much, you quickly get distracted and meditation loses its control.

1.5 Moving Meditation

Walking exercise is an excellent type of exercise, and not just beginner counseling. The aim of this mediation technique is to practice caution. This requires a lot of time, but for those of artistic minds and imagination who want to learn how to settle down and focus their thinking it is really good. There is no special form of performing exercise on walking. This form of meditation can encourage deep attention, concentration or interpretation, based on how you do it.

To beginners, an effective fitness strategy is to rely on their own walking. How does it get you started? While only walking and focusing on your own walking may sound straightforward, you may notice that it's actually really difficult.

You'll find a quiet place to move to go so that you won't be disturbed or annoyed. Walking may sound quite strange, particularly for other people. And maybe you want to choose a spot you won't be seen in. This might not be the best way to meditate at home but feel free to do so if your home has enough space.

Only stay there for a minute or two, take a deep breath and give your energy to your body, before you begin to meditate. Ideally you will meditate for a total of 15 minutes. The pace of your walk is supposed to be steady and smooth. When your mind is irritated, or your capacity to concentrate is restricted, calm down so that in the current moment you can proceed on any step.

1.6 Qigong Meditation

Qigong is a traditional Chinese ritual meant to merge the mind, and body together. They use the force known as Qi (pronounced "chi") to put the three into order. Qigong treatment can be done in two ways: in slow motion, seated or lying.

Two forms of Qi energy exist: Yin (silent and sitting) and Yang (active movements).

Qigong involves many separate movements, frequently with complex mouth and body postures. You could have hurt yourself, because you don't realize what you're doing. For this purpose, we recommend that you visit a professional trainer or continue with basic poses first, in order to produce the strongest outcomes.

Qigong therapy is the perfect type of exercise for someone who wants to seek out meaningful and functional treatment.

1.7 Chakra Meditation

Chakras are the body's energy-centers that begin at the base of the spine and stretch up to the top of the head. The body

consists of seven great chakras, each is referring to a particular trait of our personality.

Chakra therapy works at stabilizing and harmonizing all energy centers. This is therefore appropriate for those who seek moral and physical recuperation. This form of meditation is part of the dream therapy section which is why it fits anyone who loves very intensive visualization meditations.

The best way to do chakra meditation is to take controlled meditation. Step by step guided meditations are ideal for chakra meditations, especially if you have never operated with the chakra method before. It may be difficult to recall the colors and roles of each Chakra.

1.8 Recommended Meditation

In fact, prescribed therapy is a modern method. This mediation technique is certainly the best way to do the mediation, particularly for beginners. One advises some kind of contemplation, as the name implies. Provided therapy, of the essence, is a spoken lesson.

A step-by-step guided practice can make sense in several respects. This is well for newcomers as this "brings you alive" at regular intervals and focuses the attention on the essential moment, the current moment. It is also appropriate not just for learners but also for advanced students who choose to concentrate on different approaches or have difficulties.

1.9 Mantra Meditation

Mantra meditation is a type of mantras-focusing meditation. Mantras are religious words and phrases, or any phrase conveying a meaning of peace and harmony.

The meditation on the mantra is old. They were initially of Hindu heritage and were related to other gods and creeds. Today they focus mainly on spirituality. Some exercise is simple to perform, and is therefore suitable for everyone. That provides a sense of peace and harmony for the students. To perform a mantra meditation you have to sit quietly and close your legs. So spend a few minutes on your breath to quiet down all the muscles in your body.

Echo the affirmation softly, until you know you are in a calm state of mind. Gradually say it, and then feel the rhythm of the term more as you exhale. Repeat chant for 10-15 minutes. Most traditional mantras are recognized as "OM," "YAM" or "RAM," although the latter is classified as chakra. This meditative form is incorrectly named OM meditation.

1.10 Open Consciousness Meditation

Broad Awareness Meditation is a meditation process in which you open your mind to explore something around you, without concentrating on anything significant. That is in relation to concentrative counseling.

They view that all the more critically and don't pay mind to it. This may be daunting to others, particularly at the beginning. The mind is focused on evaluating objects and understanding them. You have to have a really relaxed mind to be fully present without constraints and directions.

Therefore in this form of contemplation the mind is compared to an open sky. The specialist tests the clouds (pensées) in motion. Meditation on the free mind is a stronger form of meditation, opposed to a guided meditation. Zazen meditation and vipassana meditation are free awareness meditations, for example.

Once, if you openly meditate it means you set your mind open. Or put it another way, you let all that occurs float out. You only are conscious of all that is going on and you don't evaluate, examine or prioritize everything.

Strictly put, this is the true essence of contemplation. All modern forms of meditation recognize that focusing on an occurrence or the mechanism of recording is simply means of training the mind. This enables the entrance into inner harmony and a deeper condition of consciousness.

1.11 Want to Meditate Thoroughly?

First, there's no decent treatment like that. So instead of asking yourself how to meditate correctly, are you trying to talk about how to meditate effectively?

You should then look at the concept of brain waves and figure out how meditation functions and what happens to the mind and body during meditation. You need to know which brain wave stands for which state of mind for better-using therapy.

Of starters, if you want to overcome your fears, discover your creative part or work on your sleep issues, you need to incorporate specific forms of therapy in each situation. It is how you have to cope with each condition with a single brain wave.

The first step of meditation 101 is to understand brain waves and the resulting brain conditions to produce the desired results effectively.

Waves of the brain and Meditation

Regardless of the state of mind the brain functions at different brain stages. That state of mind, such as pleasure, tension, or relaxation, has a prevalent brainwave frequency that defines it.

A safe meditation for beginners is to concentrate on one's own heart. This is actually the easiest way to move from the Alpha or Beta state to the Theta state. The body and mind function in tandem and when the body rhythm is weaker the brain waves can slow down along with it.

Alpha Waves

Within the frequency range the alpha waves fly between 8 and 13 Hertz. They are "the power of the moment" and bring harmony and tranquility. Your brain typically runs on alpha waves when you're performing your meditation or mindfulness.

These brain waves facilitate fitness, calmness, vision, communication with mind and body, and comprehension.

Beta Waves

Beta waves in a frequency range move between 13 and 38 Hertz, and represent the normal waking state. Those show about as you take on something that is physically taxing. The beta-waves are also correlated with fear and depression.

Theta Waves

Theta waves vary from 4 to 7 Hertz and are correlated with strong perception and relaxing during sleep. Theta brain waves arise very frequently when you sleep, most also as you turn them into a deep trance. The theta condition is a semi-consciousness that normally only fleetingly triggers when you get up or are about to fall asleep.

You are in a dream, you are in Theta. You perceive animated images outside the human conscience, and have a vibrant imagination.

Delta Waves

Delta waves dropped below 4 Hertz, are similar to theta waves that arise throughout the entire sleep cycle. This brain wave shape is slow, which moves within a very narrow frequency range. We arrive in quiet contemplation, and nap. Under this state, it causes healing and regeneration. That is why healthy and restful sleep is so essential to the healing process.

Gamma Waves

The gamma waves are mostly unexplored brain waves that pass between 39 and 100 Hertz in a frequency spectrum. They are present mainly during higher mental tasks and higher cognitive vision states. Would that mean certain forms of brain waves are stronger than others? The conclusion lies in no. Every wave in the brain has a different role.

You may choose to generate a specific brain wave more frequently in the course of the day, depending on the time and operation. That needs some power, versatility, and resilience.

Chapter 2: Meditation in Children.

Children have wild minds, and remain out of control much of the time, jumping from here to there at will. The easiest method of controlling their monkey mind is by diligent contemplation. Children's therapy is really effective as it helps children lead a happier existence and the support they seek to succeed in their lives. With the increased stress and academic success, children can get a variety of health-related problems. Those involve stress, anxiety, heart-related conditions and other mental and physical problems that require care with urgent effect. There's no safer therapy than sleep in a child's growth phase. Child therapy, at every level of development, allows them less violent, more concentrated and happier.

2.1 Meditation helps to regulate feelings

The person who learns how to regulate feelings earned half the wars of life. While maintaining the stages of rough life, your child must understand the difference between various

emotions. Meditation helps children to create a rhythm that is healthy in coping with all sorts of emotions. It also allows it easy for them to perform things of life.

2.2 Meditation holds depression in place

Children are more vulnerable to anxiety, as compared to adults, so as a parent, you have to ensure sure your child is safe from any possibility of stress. The only thing that might change is meditational exercises. Meditation helps children to turn their minds away from the demands of education, while they concentrate on life. Throughout meditation, the children's bodies come under certain circumstances that are critical for both physical and mental wellbeing.

2.3 Self-fulfillment

Realizing the inner self can take years but early therapy will reward your kids with better performance. With real passion and commitment, they can determine their worth and can reflect on life.

2.4 Sure-shot approaches to teach the children mediation skills

Here we discuss some meditation skills approaches for the children's;

Be a mentor to them

To encourage your family, don't only ask your family to meditate, but be their mentor and practice the same mediation process.

This would help you create a win-win scenario, because your kids would be motivated to meditate, so you will still reap meditation benefits. When you don't know how to meditate effectively, perhaps you should start watching some YouTube videos or attending a meditation center for your kids.

Let's be careful

Children consider it overwhelming to learn the yoga practice, since they are not trained mentally and psychologically for it! Work with them in a friendly manner, and let them learn the techniques of meditation. Bear in mind that you help them become a better human being, and that your abusive acts can leave their minds scarred.

Begin by breathing

Don't dwell on the nature of counseling on the very first day, as it can put the children in a state of agitation so they will be easily tuned out. Begin your day-one with general breathing, and show your children the proper way to relax their bodies through meditation.

Transform it into a fun session

The easiest way to make the children learn to meditate is by making it an enjoyable experience. No wonder, kids enjoy fun-filled events. Recite the meditation stories of certain fun children or touch their minds before you continue meditating.

2.5 Few child-friendly calming strategies to create a balance of fun and happiness

The best tool for soothing infants and small children is body screening. What you have to do is hold your mind occupied about something so you can forget all the body-pains, fatigue

and all the other issues that are running in your mind. Learning the way to meditate can be overwhelming if you practice an incorrect approach. These are the best calming methods that can benefit them.

Take the representative

When you have an adult kid that is more than five years of age so use the main counseling method you will operate seamlessly. Ask your children to imitate you and say the same things as you do. This should help them appreciate the lesson, while ensuring a healthy bond between parent and child to encourage them. When a kid learns something about his / her father, it is better to be yourself the teacher.

Take a meditation pad to lie down and allow the kids to stay peacefully in there. Encourage them to shut their windows, when relying on the water. Call on them to begin counting their breaths.

Say the Mantras

Chanting mantras offers tremendous benefits for the body as well as the soul. This is also a method of mediation widely utilized around the globe. Learn and practice some mantras with your family.

You should use audio mantras and the best soothing music to help children develop audibility and keep the children alert as necessary. Singing the mantras will make them stronger, safer and more negative-immune.

2.6 How can you encourage children to meditate?

Meditation teaching may be neck pain if you follow an old

 approach that does not motivate the students. Children look out for things that they consider intriguing. And you have to make counseling equally fun and pleasant for youth.

Hold meditation quick and convenient

Never go into detail while doing meditation with your family. Your aim will be to help them practice the art of meditation, not to keep them alive. Use common terms to allow people to grasp what you're thinking about.

Enable them to meditate on movements

Meditation is easy when you are assisting the kids with movements. Physical gestures are more capable of drawing attention, and more successful than verbal strategies.

Render it their daily routine

Motivate the kid to do fitness on a regular basis, and help him make it his routine. Set the schedule appropriately, and maintain a time slot for rehearsal. They are going to do it by themselves before they are able to practice meditation.

Creating a meditative setting

The children will never focus on sleep until their rooms are packed with sports. Ensure the atmosphere is clear from obstructions and is clean enough to guarantee sanitation.

See the best lessons for children on meditation

While supporting your children with the practice of yoga you ought to keep reminding yourself. See any videos and learn the methods for sustaining a sense of enjoyment in meditation.

Place them aside

Kids hate the restrictions, so you will set them free for a moment during the healing period. Begin or finish your meditation with a friendly game of play and make the children go home. We will be more involved and if you allow them to relax throughout the session we will react to you with improved performance.

2.7 Meditation for Children and Mothers – The Latest BFFs

Will you think children are nowadays barely loud? Ah, well, they're all focused on playing sports, watching smartphones and videos. What time to practice, when clever machine machines use up all of their resources! Is the little one still caught on the phone too? All right, this isn't all about your kid alone. Nowadays, nearly all children find it very challenging to wriggle out of their addiction to gadgets, because technology is almost everywhere. And this scares parents to no end! Talking of how to pull them out of this modern age pit, did you plan to subject your child to meditation?

By encouraging children's exercise they can restore their innate capacity to focus. Meditation tends to increase levels of self-esteem and confidence, and also creates empathy among adolescents. If this seems like a good concept to you then follow this tutorial to bring your family to meditation.

How Long Will Children Meditate?

A significant aspect of children's therapy practice is that you ought to keep the process as pleasurable and enjoyable as possible.

Make sure the process isn't monotonous, or their focus will probably fade quite soon. To make things more fun you'll care for the senses and imagination of the little people. But be sure that you don't plan too long -the timing is just as vital to maintaining for them to be fun and exciting. You have to continue with a few minutes a day, five minutes would be a good start. It is quite challenging for children to obtain the requisite concentration during counseling, so hopefully five minutes will help in the initial level.

Over time, and dependent on the infant's rate of development, you can keep growing the period at a slow, calculated level. The primary objective is to create a schedule so that there is no point in drawing time by manipulation which will eventually exacerbate the child's aversion to meditation. Take them on fast.

Okay, what is the actual length it should be?

You do not want your kid to meditate intentionally for 20 minutes like an adult, to be practical. Kids are accustomed to actively moving the focus from one dimension to the next. The usage of modern technologies also means that individuals have a usually reduced attention spectrum.

Experts also believe that a children's counseling session will ideally be one greater than their age. For e.g., if your child is eight years old then aim to do a session of 9 minutes. This way, you won't test their stamina easily and build space smartly for another session again. And again, as mentioned above, proceed at a slow and calculated pace over time.

Seek imagination with them

You could ask them to place a gadget on their tummy instead of asking them to "look at your air," for example, and watch it go up and down. You should maybe urge them to seek to move issues as quickly as possible. You would have taught them, without understanding, how to breathe deeply in this way.

How do you soothe a crying child?

Maybe the most dreaded task for any parent is to seek to comfort a gruesome child! Yet with certain points in mind, you will easily have this done.

Engage in Calming Sports

Let them think it's cool if they decide to take a couple of minutes 'rest. That could mean making them do what they like, including painting, reading a book. You can always engage them in listening to the music that they find good. In the end, it will shift their emphasis and make them calm down. You should have the best calming music to hold children in charge of their moods.

Manage what they're subjected to

Everything a kid thinks is always getting a huge impact on their behavior. When you experience threats on social media, make sure you delete them instantly. Providing an illustration is often necessary to educate them. When you can't contain your own anger, they can of course profit from you. And you do need to be vigilant about your own behaviors and actions.

2.8 When and why are moms expected to meditate with kids?

Meditation is a therapeutic activity that is really powerful. The relationship would be more strengthened if you and your kid participate together. You'll feel like you're developing together and cultivating a loving mother-child partnership.

There would also be significant positive changes in your lives. They'll be able to perform well at school with cognitive therapy for girls. Children will also gain the capacity to manage their emotions better, and use a logical mind to make reasonable judgments.

When you want your child to get accustomed to meditation, it is better to start with children while they are very small with a gentle morning meditation. As they grow older, they'll be used to living this way. You can also encourage them to try yoga later on with you.

2.9 What's the right way to practice meditation with your children?

Bedtime meditations are very helpful in elevating the stress rates of the infant. It is generally accepted that a child should be able to meditate, relative to their age, for a duration of minutes. But if mom can really get her kid to bed, it will last longer, and hopefully help them sleep better.

Two of the main conditions are relaxing environments in your child's sleep, such as mellow illumination and calming music. He / her children should read reading stories too. So you should keep doing this therapeutic process and children can cope more frequently for a successful outcome.

2.10 What research shows about Meditation in kids?

Carefulness-meditation approaches have proven useful in diagnosing various psychological disorders such as chronic pain, diet issues, insomnia and anxiety, according to studies since the early 1980s. In addition to its health effects, and a growing body of research centered on assessing the cognitive consequences that continue to emerge from this form of cognitive / behavioral conditioning strategy. Accordingly, the carefulness approach of "observe and consent" has been stated to enhance the executive's working and the capacity to maintain focus.

Until now, the majority of carefulness-meditation research has concentrated on adults, although involvement in children and teenagers has just recently increased. Preliminary studies into this fledgling area suggest that planning for carefulness-meditation has positive results on children and adolescents 'psychological wellbeing. However, the overall research status is still small, especially in primary school years and healthy children.

To date, the limited research group researching the effect of carefulness-meditation planning on adolescents has documented beneficial effects of this approach in relieving tension, preventing suicidal relapse, decreasing distress and depressive symptoms, and minimizing the symptoms of Attention-Deficit / Hyperactivity Disorder (ADHD). According to the study carefulness-meditation training provided to children was shown to be successful in minimizing anxiety symptoms, growing self-compassion and communication abilities, improving social engagement, coping strategies, and decreasing ADHD symptoms, and improving behavioral regulation, meta-cognition, and executive efficiency. Of note, if one believes that problems with executive functioning are related to cognitive disorders and specific psychological conditions such as ADHD, as well as violence and delinquency, then the above study appears to be especially relevant. Apart from work on carefulness-meditation methods in school-age children, it is worth exploring current programs aimed at incorporating elements of carefulness into a social-emotional learning system (SEL) in the area of school psychology. In this regard, it is indicated that the integration of awareness of existing school-wide SEL programs may improve the efficiency of the whole program with regard to disadvantaged children's social and emotional capacities. This may also enable students to stay concentrated and positive, and be especially helpful in preventing disciplinary issues. Although highly helpful, the aforementioned work on carefulness-meditation methods in adolescents has a number of disadvantages. Most of these studies did not employ any control group, control group waiting list, control group quiet reading, or control group receptive monitoring. In addition, children were typically required to meditate along with teachers and/or parents in these studies and the evaluation of the effect of carefulness-meditation on children's safety and behavior was primarily based on parent and instructor experiences. The statistical problem may be that the reported changes were exaggerated simply because they had already participated in the counseling phase (i.e., inflation / placebo effect). There is no previous work comparing the experiences of parents and teachers (compiled before and after intervention or not with babies) to the self-reported findings of teens, to the best of our knowledge in this regard. Finally, some of the previous care-based solutions for young people were done for middle and high school students. Nevertheless, only a few studies involved younger children in the first years of high school. Furthermore, one of these three studies was conducted without a control group on a specific pediatric sample of 5 anxious children (7–8 years), while the other two tests were conducted in non-clinical samples that did not have appropriate surveillance procedures.

Roy Hintsa, an MBSR organizer based in Toronto, Canada, says it is necessary to encourage children to care so that they can deal with tension more comfortably in puberty. One useful recommendation from Hintsa is that younger children "are more apt to react to physical activity," so he advises that young children be given respiratory therapy by letting them lie down and keep their beloved stuffed toy in their hands. He further notes that children of all ages respond better to the teachings of mindfulness if the entire family is active, and he advises that parents practice mindfulness by offering home-based sessions of mindfulness even short ones. It may also have the additional benefit of encouraging parents to spend time in relaxation on their own meditation practice.

Chapter 3: Meditation Stories for Kids

Using the influence of mediation on mindfulness and a fun, soothing tale of camping adventure, this bedtime tale is specifically crafted to help children fall asleep easily whilst giving them important life lessons of empathy and compassion. The narrator's voice will inspire their ingenuity as they unwind at the end of the day, letting them develop imagery and imagination skills.

Meditation has been found to provide a broad variety of effects for adults and adolescents, including imagination enhancing, depression aid, tension relief, and many more. Kids of all ages would enjoy hearing this tale of bedtime when they know how to make friends better and develop patience for the people around them. The meditation stories for children are allegorical, and come from the tales of Buddhist Jataka. We make good reading and the kids will love to listen.

This bedtime tale would be:

* Help Children Relax

Settle Down, and Fall Asleep Quicker

* Inspire Imagination

* Teach Children about Empathy, Kindness, and Having New Friends

* Help Them Exercise Dreaming

* Leave Them Recharged For the Next Day

3.1 Feast for the Dead

While in Benares, a brahmin, who was well versed in the four Vedas, decided to give the dead a feast. He told his pupils to fetch a goat and instructed them, "Bring this goat down to the river, bathe it, put a wreath around his neck, and carry it back." "Very good," replied the pupils, and took the goat down to the river, where they bathed and garlanded it, and placed it down on the bank. By the force of recalling her past lives, the goat was mindful of her actions in those lives and was overjoyed at this day's thinking of being freed from all its suffering. It was crying loudly like a kettle was breaking. Instead the goat had deep remorse for the brahmin by murdering him, enduring the same pain that he himself had suffered, and wept with a loud voice. "Dear goat," the amazed young pupils questioned, "what makes you laugh and cry at the same time?" "Tell me this query before your lord." And they took the goat to the brahmin, and told him about it. The brahmin, having heard the tale, told the goat why it was laughing and why it was crying. So the goat talked to the brahmin, "O brahmin, I, like you, was a brahmin in the past, well versed in the ancient vedas, offering a feast for the dead, killed a goat for my offering; and by killing that single goat, I had my head cut off five hundred times, all but one. That's my five hundredth and last birth; and I laughed loudly when I learned that this very day I'm going to be burning.

The goat said, "On the other side, I wept, knowing that although I, who was destined to lose my head five hundred times, was being freed from my suffering today, you will be condemned to a similar fate as a punishment for killing me. Therefore, I wept for you out of sympathy." "Do not be scared, goat," the brahmin said. "I'm not going to harm you." "Why do you mean this is brahmin?" the goat asked. "I can't avoid death today if you destroy me or not." "Don't be scared, goat, I'll go with you to defend you." "Poor is your defense, brahmin and powerful is the power of my past evil-doing."

Setting the goat loose, the brahmin said to his followers, "Let's not let someone harm this goat." He agreed to pursue the goat closely with his pupils around him.

This stretched out its neck as soon as the goat was able to graze at the leaves of a bush rising on top of a hill. And a lightning bolt hit the rock at that very moment, tearing off a sharp fragment that cut through the outstretched neck of the goat and beheaded the poor beast.

During those days the boddhisattva was raised in the very same place as a 'tree divinity.' He now looked to all those who had gathered there, sitting cross-legged in mid-air.

He said to him, "If these beings understood only the fruit of doing bad, they could desist from murdering." He then told them the Fact, "If people but understood the reality that their lives are suffering, and then living things might cease to take life. Here is the end of the slayer."

3.2 The Discontented Ox

When in Benares the boddhisattva was brought to life as an ox in a farmer's household.

The boddhisattva had a younger nephew, the miserable ox and they did all the family's draught-work together.

The farmer had a lovely daughter, and a rich landlord demanded her hand for his young son in the union.

Being bad, the farmers' family began fattening the pig they owned in order to prepare a dainty feast for the wedding guests.

Observing this, the younger ox said to his elder brother, "When you and I get half of this family's tons, we get to consume just straw and grass while this pig is fed rice every day for doing nothing. What's the explanation for the pig getting handled so well?" The older ox replied, "Don't envy him, my good boy, for the pig consumes the food of death. The family feeds the pig to give joy at the wedding of their daughter. Wait, just a little longer, then the visitors will arrive. Then you can see the pig lugged out, slaughtered, then placed at the table for the visitors to consume." He added, "Don't envy the pig, he consumes this misery.

The boddhisattva said to the younger ox, "Do you see the tragedy that afflicted the pig, dear brother?" "I saw the effect of the feasting of the pig. Better than a hundred, nay a thousand times that such food is ours, while it's just hay, chaff and straw- so our feed doesn't hurt us, so it's a promise that our lives won't be cut short."

3.3 The Fowler and the Quails

The boddhisattva once had been raised as a quail and worked in the forest as the leader of thousands of quails.

A fowler, who came to capture quails, used to mimic a quail's message to bring the birds together. Instead he threw his net over them at once to collect them all before returning home to market them for a living.

Observing this, the boddhisattva said to the quails, "This fowler wreaks havoc on our kinsfolk. I have a way to avert capture, so you will all work together to make it a success. In the future, if the fowler throws the net over you, put your head out of the mesh and travel away to a thorn bush where we will all hide." "We're going to do it properly really well," they all responded.

The next day they did only what the boddhisattva had told them to do when the net was flung over them. They raised the net up and lowered it into a thorn bush, fleeing from below.

After wasting hours disengaging his net from the bush the fowler had to return empty-handed. The quails served together for the day-after-day to foul the intentions of the fowler and the fellow has little to show for his actions on coming home. With the sudden failure his wife became restless and furious.

The fowler explained to his friend, "The quails are now working together-the moment I throw my net over them, they run off with it and drop it on a thorn-bush to flee. However, they do not exist in harmony. I do bag them again as soon as they start bickering among themselves." He also sang softly,

"When concord reigns, the birds carry off the nest; when quarrels emerge, the birds fall victim to the nest; not long ago one of the quails mistakenly jumped on the head of another and a fight erupted. They bandied threats, and relentlessly taunted one another.

The boddhisattva, who observed from a distance, said to himself, "There is no peace for one who is quarrelsome. The time has arrived when they can no longer pick up the net to carry on their own demise. I will no longer remain here."

Shortly afterwards, the fowler came back and drew them by imitating a quail's voice, and when they had assembled, he cast his net over them.

Instead of running, one quail said to the other, "They claim, while you were at work raising the net, the hair from your head dropped off; now is your moment, raise it off." The other responded, "They claim, while you lifted the net, both of your wings were molten; now is your moment, raise it off." However, when they were exhorting each other to lift the net, the fowler raised the net for them, stuffed it into a basket.

3.4 The Fish Who Worked a Miracle

Once upon a time in northern India the Enlightened Being was raised as a fish in a sea. There were many forms of fish, big and small, with the Bodhisatta residing in the water.

A time of extreme draught has come to pass. The rainy season hasn't been as normal. The men's crops perished, and filled out several wetlands, streams, and waterways.

The fish and tortoises dug down and submerged themselves in the water, seeking frenzied to hold them clean and to save. And that had delighted the crows. They put their beaks in the water, picked the frightened little fish out and feasted on them.

The other fish's agony of misery and death badly touched the Enlightened Man, and filled him with remorse and empathy. He knew he was the only one willing to help them. But we'd like a miracle.

The reality was he'd remained innocent. By never destroying anyone's property. He was eager to use the strength of this wholesome reality to allow rain to fall from the sky and free from their misery and death his family.

He pushed himself from under the black dirt. He was a large trout, and brushed ebony as deep from the mud as. He opened his arms, gleaming like rubies, stared up to the sky and named Pajjunna the rain god. He shouted, "Oh my friend Pajjunna, god of rain, I suffer for my relatives' sake. How do you deprive me of rain, which is totally free, and make me struggle with all these fish?" He pushed himself from under the black dirt. He was a large trout, and brushed ebony as deep from the mud as. He opened his arms, gleaming like rubies, stared up to the sky and named Pajjunna the rain god. He cried, "Oh my friend Pajjunna, god of rain, I suffer for my relatives' sake. Why should you prevent me from raining, which is perfectly healthy, and make me suffer in solidarity with all these animals?" "I was born among fish, for which it is common to consume other animals - including our own sort, like cannibals! Yet since I was raised, I have never eaten any fish, including one   as   tiny   as   rice! And he started, ordering the great rain god Pajjunna: "Have rain fall from the thunderclouds! Don't make the crows feel their secret jewels! Let the crows feel the shame of their sinful acts. At the same time free me from my misery, which existed in complete wholesomeness." After a brief pause, the heavens opened with a massive storm, relieving all of them from the terror of d. And when finally the big fish that had performed this magic expired, he was resurrected as he deserved.

3.5 The Strong-Minded Snake

There once was a psychiatrist who had been a specialist in the care of snakebites. One day the family of a man who was attacked by a lethal poisonous snake called for him.

"There are two methods to handle this snake bite," the doctor told them. "One is by offering medication. The other is by catching the snake that bit him and getting him to suck out his own venom." The family replied, "We'd like to catch the snake and have him suck the venom out." After the snake was found, the doctor asked him, "Did you bite this man?" "Yes I did," the snake answered. "Alright then," said the doctor, "you will suck your own poison out of the bite." But the strong-willed snake answered, "Taking back my own poison? No! I know I did such a thing and I never will!" So the doctor ignited a wood fire and said to the snake, "If you don't suck the poison out, I'll throw you into this fire and roast you up!" Yet the snake had agreed. He said, "I'd like to die!" And he began running towards the flames.

The specialist snake-bite doctor has never seen anything like this in all his years! He took mercy on the noble dog, and stopped him from joining the fire. He used his drugs and healing spells to cure the man who was dying from the toxin.

The doctor appreciated the resolve of a single-minded serpent. He realized he might better himself if he exercised his ambition in a wholesome manner. Therefore, he showed him the Five Steps of Learning to prevent inappropriate acts. He then set him free, stating, "Go in grace, and bring no harm to anyone."

3.6 Fresh Houses for the Spirits of the Plant (Wise Council)

The King of the Tree Spirits once died as happens to all things. King Sakka, Heaven lord of 33, named a new King of the Spirits of the Forest. The new King sent out a declaration as to his first official act that every tree spirit should choose a tree in which to reside. Likewise it was mentioned that each tree should be satisfied with its spirit of residence. There also happened to be a very wise spirit of the tree which was the chief of a large clan. He also told leaders of his community not to stay among standing woods. Instead, staying in the forest woods around him will be better. The wise spirits of the tree lived together with their chief among the woodland woods. Yet there were some stupid and greedy spirits in the forest as well. They said to each other, "Why would we stay in this crowd? Let's go to the human-inhabited settlements, towns and cities. Tree spirits that dwell there get the finest gifts, and they're still revered by the superstitious citizens that reside in those areas. What an existence we're going to have!" So they went to the communities, towns and cities and migrated into the large free-standing forests, cared for. Suddenly, a major storm rolled up that day.

The wind blows fast and heavy. Throughout the storm the large strong trees with aged brittle roots were not doing well. Branches have collapsed, trunks have snapped in two, and others have also been uprooted. Yet in the immense storm, the trees in the wood, entangled with each other, were able to bend and support one another. They didn't slip or crack! The tree spirits had their tree homes demolished in communities, towns, and counties. They collected their kids and went back into the wood. We are moaning to the wise leader about their suffering in the great lonely trees of men's soil. He said, "This is what happens to those reckless, who disregard wise advice and go out on their own."

3.7 Four on a Log (Gratitude)

King Brahmadatta of Benares once had one sibling. He grows up to be a mean and ruthless he-man-the kind who often wants to show that he is better than anyone else. He was a brute who was always throwing people around, stirring up battles. This was through a flood of obscenities any time he talked to them-straight out of the gutter. And he'd also been able to get upset-almost like a hissing snake that's just got on. People hid from him inside and outside the building, like they might from a man-eating monster that was starving. We rejected him, like a speck of dirt in their eyes. All dubbed him the 'Dark Prince' behind his back. In short-he wasn't a handsome man! The prince wanted to go for a dip that day. And he and his servants and attendants fell to the water. It all of a sudden became almost as dark as night. It was a big hurricane. The prince was also able to prove, being so rough and gritty, that he was not scared of something. So he yelled at his staff, "Take me into the center of the water to bathe me. And get me back to the sea." They brought him out to the midstream following his instructions. And they said, "Whatever we do here, the king can never find out. But let's destroy the Evil Prince. You go into the flood, good-for-nothing!" They plunged him into the stormy, roaring water. The others inquired, when they returned to the house, where the prince was. They responded, "We don't know. Because the rain came up, he would swim quicker than us to go back to Benares." Once they returned to the palace, the king said, "Where is my son?" They answered, "We don't know, your majesty. When the storm came up, we figured he was heading back in front of us." They diligently hunted; all the way to the riverside, but couldn't locate him. It was that thing that had occurred. The prince had been washed down the raging river in darkness and wind and storm. He was thankfully able to reach a falling, decaying tree root. He kept on for dear life in a desperate way. The strong he-man was so scared of sinking when he was being carried along, that he screamed like a frightened powerless boy! It only occurred that a really wealthy guy had died in Benares, not long ago. At the riverbank, in the same line of the river, he had hidden his treasure cache. His wealth was approximately 40 million gold coins. He was resurrected as a lowly serpent, slithering on his belly while still protecting his fortune because of his wretched lust for wealth. Another wealthy miser has hidden a cache of 30 million gold coins at a neighboring location on the riverbank. And he had been resurrected as a water rat because of his stingy clawing for money. He kept on protecting his hidden treasure too. Lo hey and behold. Around the moment of the hurricane, both the snake and the rat were flushed from their holes and swept into the rushing water. They all happened to hold onto the same dead log holding the terrified wailing boy, in danger of drowning. The snake climbed to one hand and the water rat to the other.

A big cotton tree has also happened to rise nearby. This housed a teenage parrot roosting. When the storm-flooded river rose up, the roots of the cotton tree were swept away and it sunk into the sea. As he wanted to fly down, the wind and rain with the worm, the water rat and the Evil Prince washed the little parrot onto the same dead tree.

 The four of them start walking in the river into a curve. A holy man was staying humbly in a little hut nearby. He actually happens to be the Bodhisatta-the Person of the Awakening. He was born into a rich, high-class family in Kasi. He had given up both his money and place when he had grown up, and had come to live by himself across the water. It was midnight before the Holy Man received the scream of alarm from the Evil Duke. He said, "That sounds like a scared

 human being. My goodness and caring won't let me neglect him. I have to save him." He went down to the river and cried. "Don't be afraid! I'll save you!" Then he leapt into the raging river, caught the log, and pulled it to shore with great strength.

He safely helped the prince walk onto the riverbank. He found the lizard, rat of water and parrot, and brought them to his cozy little house, along with the man. He began the fire to cook. Thinking of the animals' vulnerability he warmed them gently by the flames. He put them aside when they'd been warm and dry. Then, he let himself warm the prince. The saintly man brought out several fruits and nuts. He again first fed the more vulnerable creatures, followed by the Prince who was waiting. It made the Evil Prince not shockingly angry! He thought, "This dumb holy man doesn't care about me at all, a wonderful royal prince. Instead he gives these three dumb animals a higher position!" Thinking that way, he built up vengeful hate towards the benevolent Bodhisatta. The spiritual guy dried out the deadwood log in the light the following day. He then chopped it up and burned it, frying their food and holding it dry. The four saved by the same log became solid and stable within a few days. The snake came to say good-bye to the saintly one. He coiled his body to the table, arched himself, and politely bowed his head. He said, "Venerable man, you've done a wonderful deal for me! I'm thankful to you, and I'm not a bad snake. I've got a hidden fortune of 40 million gold coins in some spots, and I'll happily give it to you-it's invaluable for all life! If you're in need of capital, just come down to the bank of the river and call out. "Snake! Cat!-Snake! "The water mouse, too, had come to say farewell to the holy guy. He sat on his hind legs, and politely lowered his head. He said," Venerable sir, you have done me a wonderful job! Thank you and I'm not a bad water rodent. I've got a hidden fortune of 30 million gold coins, somewhere. And I'll gladly give this to you-it's invaluable for all creation! Whenever you need capital, just get down on the bank of the river and call out, "Rat! Rat!" O respectful kindness from a river rat and a worm! A long cry from their stingy human existence then! Then the parrot came to say good-bye to the saintly one. He bowed his head politely and said, "Venerable sir, you've done a wonderful deal for me! I'm thankful to you, but I don't have any silver or gold. I'm not a bad parrot, though; for if you're ever in need of the finest rice, just come down to the bank of the river and call out. 'Parrot! Parrot!' Then I'll collect all my relatives from all the Himalayan woods, and we'll get you ma' since his mind was loaded with revenge venom, he was only contemplating murdering him if he ever saw him again. What he meant, though, was, "Venerable man, please come to me. If I am the King and the Four Necessities I must give to you." He came back to Benares and eventually became the new king.

The holy man has resolved in a while to see if these four's loyalty is for real. He first dropped to the bank of the river and cried out, "Snake! Snake!" The snake crawled out of his house under the ground at the sound of the first word. He bowed politely and replied, "Dear god, 40 million gold coins are hidden beneath this very place. Dig them up and carry them with you!" "Oh good," the holy man answered, "I must come again when I am in need." After the snake's leave, he marched

down the side of the river and cried out,' "Rat! Rat!" The water-rat emerged, and it all continued on as it had with the lizard.

Then he cried out, "Parrot! Parrot!" The parrot flew down from his treetop house, bowed politely, and said, "Holy one, do you need red rice? I'll invite my family, and we'll carry you the best rice in all the Himalayas." The holy man said, "Well, when I'm in need I'll come again." He stepped into the royal garden of fun, and stayed there overnight. In the morning he went to receive alms food in the city of Benares, in a rather modest and dignified way.

The ungrateful monarch, seated on a magnificently decorated royal elephant, led a large parade through town that same morning. As he noticed the Enlightenment Being approaching from a distance, he said, "Aha! This poor street bum is going to sponge me off. Until he may brag to others how much he has accomplished for me, I will make him beheaded!" So he said to his servants, "This useless mendicant will come and ask for something. Don't let the good-for-nothing come near me. Unlike a growing thief they bound the blameless Great Being. On the road to the execution block they whipped him mercilessly at every corner of the street. Yet no matter how rough they beat him, he stayed dignified, digging through his skin. After every whipping he plainly declared, for everyone to hear: "This shows that the old proverb is still real - 'There is more satisfaction in dragging deadwood out of a river than in supporting an ungrateful man!'" Some of the spectators started asking why he said this at every corner of the path. They said to each other, "An ungrateful man will trigger the suffering of this poor man." And they asked him, "Oh holy lord, have you done an ungrateful man?" Then he told them the whole story. And in addition he said, "I saved this king from an awful storm, and in so doing I put this misery upon myself that I did not obey the old wise's saying, which is That is why I meant what I was doing." When the citizens of Benares learned this story, they were angry and said to each other, 'This good guy saved

—

65

the king's life. But he's so mean he has almost no love in him. What will a king like that actually help us? He can be only harmful to us. Let's just get him! "Their anger turned the people of Benares into a crowd. They attacked the king with bullets, sticks, clubs and bricks. He died while still seated on the imperial elephant. And they tossed the dead body of the ancient Evil Prince into a pit by the side of the road. So they declared the holy man their new ruler. Benares governed well. But one day he wanted to go and see his old friends. Cat!-Snake! "The snake came out, showed appreciation, and said, 'my god, if you so wish. The king told his workers to dig up the 40 million gold coins. He went to the house of the river rat and cried out, "Snake! Cat! Cat! "He too came, gave gratitude, and said, 'My lord, if you would, you would be welcome in my riches.' This time the king's servants dug up thirty million gold coins, and the king cried out, 'Parrot! Too much parrot! "The parrot flew to the king, bowed politely, and said, 'Should you desire, my lord, I shall collect for you the most excellent red rice.' But the king replied, 'Not my friend now. If rice is required I will ask you for it. Now let's all return to the city. "When they landed at the royal palace in Benares, The king had the Gold Coins worth 70 million put under guard in a safe place. He had a silver bowl built for the new home of the happy snake. With the gentle rat he had a maze with the finest crystals to stay in. And the loving parrot moved into a golden cage, with a gate that he could open and unlatch from within. Per day the king gave the snake and the parrot rice puffs and the sweetest bee's honey on golden plates. And he brought the water rat the most delicious scented rice on yet another golden tray.

The king was known for his kindness to the needy. For several years he and his three best companions worked together in complete peace. They were all resurrected when they expired, as they deserved.

3.8 Mr Monkey and Sir Crocodile (Good Manners)

Mr. Monkey once stayed by himself, by a riverbank. He was really heavy, and a good jumper. There was a lovely island in the center of the river which was covered with mango, jackfruit and other fruit trees. Halfway between bank and island there appeared to be a boulder sticking out of the mud. Though it appeared unlikely, Mr. Monkey was able to leap from the side of the river to the cliff, then from the cliff to the island. During the day he will consume fruit and then ride home via the same road every evening. Next to the same river a high class family sir Crocodile and Lady Crocodile were staying. They were anticipating their first baby crockery brood. Since Lady Crocodile was pregnant she occasionally wanted to consume weird things. And she made uncommon demands upon her faithful friend. Unlike the other creatures, Lady Crocodile had been shocked at the way Mr. Monkey flew back and forth to the rock. One day she spontaneously developed a desire to consume Mr. Monkey's head! She stated her wish to Sir Crocodile. He vowed to have her heart for Mr. Monkey in time for dinner, to satisfy her. Sir Crocodile went ahead and laid down on the rock between the shore of the river and the reef. He waited the evening for Mr. Monkey to arrive, hoping to capture him. Mr. Monkey has spent the majority of the day on the island, as normal. Once it was time to get back on the riverbank to his house, he found that the rock seemed to have risen. It was higher than he'd recalled above water. He studied and found that the depth of the river was the same as in the morning, but the rock was certainly bigger. He instantly accused Sir Crocodile of being clever. He yelled in the direction of the rock to find out for sure, "Hey there, Mr. Stone! How are you?" he screamed these three times. Then he yelled, "You used to address me when I talked to you, but today you're not doing something. What's wrong with you, Mr. Rock?" Sir Crocodile figured, " This rock used to converse with the monkey on certain days. I can't afford to talk with the dumb rock any longer! I'll just have to talk to the rock and fool the monkey." Then he exclaimed, "I'm good, Mr. Monkey. Which is it that you want? "Mr. Monkey said, 'Who are you? "The crocodile answered," I'm Sir Crocodile, "without thought." Why do you lie there? "The monkey persisted. Sir Crocodile replied," I'm waiting to carry your heart with you! Mr. Monkey, there's no chance for you. "The wise monkey said," Aha! He's right-the riverbank is no other route out. Now I'm going to have to fool him. "Then he exclaimed," Master Crocodile my mate, it looks like you have me. Now I'll place my hands on you. As Sir Crocodile opened his mouth, he spread it so wide that his eyes were clenched tightly. Once Mr. Monkey noticed that, he quickly leapt to the top of the head of Sir Crocodile and then instantly to the side of the water. As Sir Crocodile knew that he was outsmarted, he appreciated the triumph of Mr. Monkey. Like a true athlete in a game, he congratulated the champion. Monkey, my purpose against you was evil-I tried to destroy you, just to appease my mom. Yet you just tried to save yourself, and not hurt anybody. I always want to thank you! "And Sir Crocodile came back to Lady Crocodile. She was upset with him at first, but they overlooked their problems for a bit as the little ones arrived.

3.9 A Prince of Monkeys (Carefulness).

There was once a ruthless monkey king who had controlled the Himalayas. Within his band all the monkeys were his own wives and babies. He believed one of his sons might grow up to take over as ruler. And it was his policy right after he was raised, to bite any friend. It transformed him, such that he would feel too powerless to fight his father again. A certain Monkey King's wife became pregnant. Just in case the fetus was a baby, she tried to save him from her husband's cruel scheme. And she took off to a forest at the foot of a small mountain. She shortly carried a happy little baby boy monkey there. The kid grew up to be large and solid before long. One day he questioned his mother, "Where's my father?" She informed him, "He's the leader of a band of monkeys living at the foot of a far-off mountain. That's what makes you a kid!" The kid of monkeys said, "Take me with compassion to my family." His mother said, "No my boy, I'm scared to do that. Your family bites both his children to kill them for life. He thought when the cruel old King saw his young, powerful son. "I have no question that when my son grows stronger he will take my kingdom from me, so I have to destroy him while I can! I'll embrace him, saying it's out of affection for him, but I'll choke him down to death!" The king greeted his son, saying, "Oh, my long-lost boy! Where have you been all this time? I have desperately missed you." Then he took him in his embrace, and kissed him. He tried to pull more and more, attempting to suck all life from him! Yet monk prince was as strong as an elephant. He straight back embraced his father. He hugged him closer and closer, until he could see the rib bones of the old King beginning to crumble! After this disgusting meeting, the monkey king was much more terrified that his son would kill him one day. He said, "Nearby is a pond inhabited by a water devil. This will be easy to get him to kill my baby. And my troubles will be done!" The monkey king replied, "Hey my precious boy, now is the best time for you to come home, since I am old and I want to send you my band of monkeys, Yet I require the coronation flowers. Upon arrival at the pool, he found several kinds of water lilies and lotuses rising all over it. But rather than diving back in and sweeping them up, he was slowly researching. He moved along the street, gradually. He saw footsteps reaching the water, but none were going back! Upon realizing this, he knew it was a sure indication that a water spirit inhabited the pool. He also knew that his father needed to submit him to be murdered there. He then explored, until he discovered a small part of the marsh. There, he was able to leap straight over from one leg to the other with considerable effort. He reached down in the center of his jump and grabbed roses, without even going into the sea. He then jumped out again, picking up more seeds. He started to hop back and forth, with tons of flowers picked.

3.10 The Whatnot Tree (Prudence)

There had once been chief of the group. He had traveled from country to nation distributing various products. His caravans usually contained at least 500 carts of bullocks. His route passed through a very dense forest on one of those journeys. He named all the leaders of the caravan together before joining it. He advised them, "My boys, when you go through this wood, be cautious to avoid poisonous berries, poisonous plants, poisonous seeds, poisonous flowers and even poisonous honeycombs." Thus, anything you haven't eaten before, if it's a plant, a weed, a flower or something else, shouldn't be eaten without consulting me first. Others moved ahead of the group and overtook the tree that wasn't. They were both starving and the vegetables, which were not, looked like juicy ripe mangoes. Others suddenly began consuming the vegetables, without even noticing. Before anybody could utter a word, they devoured them. Many recalled the message from the chief so they figured this was yet another mango tree type. They felt they had the good fortune to find ripe mangoes right next to a village. And they wanted to consume some of the fruits until they all died.

Others became smarter than the others, as well. We agreed it would be better for the caravan chief to heed the warning. And if they did not know, he only happens to be the One of the Awakening. Once the leader arrived at the forest, those that were vigilant and did not consume questioned, "Leader, what is this forest? Is it possible to eat these fruits?" Upon cautiously examining, he responded, "Oh, oh. It might look like a mango tree, but it's not. It's a dangerous tree that doesn't even reach it!" Those that had already consumed the seed of what did not became frightened. The chief of the group ordered them to cough just as soon as practicable. They did this, and then four sweet foods were offered to consume-raisins, cane sugar paste, sweet yogurt and bee honey. Their taste buds were renewed in this way after vomiting up the poisonous fruit which was not. Unfortunately, it did not spare the greediest and most stupid people. They were the ones who suddenly started consuming toxic foods, without any consideration. To them it was too late. The toxin had already started to do its work, and destroyed them. In the past, as caravans arrived at whatnot vine, the inhabitants had eaten the toxic fruits and perished during the night in their beds. The first residents had appeared at the campsite the next morning. The dead bodies had been caught by the hands, pulled to a safe hiding spot, and buried. Then they had taken all of the caravan's goods and bullock carts for themselves. This time they intended to do the same. The next morning at dawn the villagers rushed for the tree which wasn't. They said to each other, "The bullocks are going to be mine!"

"I want the carts and wagons!" "I'm going to have tons of goods!" But as they approached the whatnot tree they found that much of the caravan's citizens were alive and healthy. Surprisingly, they asked, "Why do you realize it wasn't a mango tree?" They said, "We didn't know it, but our leader warned us ahead of time, so when he saw it, he knew it." So the peasants told the chief of the group, "Dear wise guy, how do you realize that this wasn't a mango tree?" He answered, "I knew that for two reasons. First, this tree is quick to ascend, and second, it's right next to a town. When the fruits on such a tree stay unpicked, they can't be healthy to eat!" Everybody was shocked that this lifesaving knowledge was based on that common meaning. The caravan was comfortably heading its journey.

3.11 A Huge Lump Of Gold (Moderation)

There was once a rich community here. The villagers' richest agreed to conceal a large lump of gold to protect against thieves and criminals. But he'd bury it in a rice field nearby.

The community was no longer prosperous several years back, and the rice field was deserted and left unused. A poor farmer started out to plow the ground. It only occurred after a while of plowing, that his plow hit the long-forgotten hidden gold.

At first he felt it had to be a really difficult root for the fruit. But when he opened it, he noticed the gold was perfect, polished. He was afraid to go to carry it with him, since it was daytime. And he once again covered it up and waited for nightfall.

The bad farmer had come back in the middle of the night. He found the golden gem again. He was able to lift it but it was too high. He put cords around her and attempted to pull her away. But he couldn't budge it an inch, it was too big. He was disappointed, feeling he was fortunate enough to discover a gem, and unfortunate enough not to be allowed to take it. He also attempted to kicke the big gold glob. Yet it didn't budge an inch yet!

So he sat back, and began to look at the case. He also wanted to divide the lump of gold into four smaller lumps. He will only be forced to take one item at a time around.

He said, "I'm going to use one lump for everyday day-to-day life. I'm going to save the second lump for a rainy day. I'm going to save the third lump in my agricultural company. Then I'm going to earn value for the fourth lump by offering it to the weak and vulnerable and for other good works." Then, bringing them home on four separate journeys was simple. He existed peacefully afterwards.

3.12 A Gang Of Drunkards (Sobriety)

The Enlightenment Being was once born in a prosperous household, when Brahmadatta was sovereign. Benares became the richest man. A gang of drunkards has even happened to be wandering the streets. All they really talked about was seeking ways to get alcohol, the substance without which they felt they could not survive. One day, they came up with a scheme to rob the richest man in Benares, although as usual they had run out of capital. But they didn't know he was the resurrected Bodhisatta, so he isn't going to be that easy to trick! They wanted to make a 'Mickey Finn' which is an alcoholic cocktail illegally applied to it from a sleeping user. They planned to have the wealthy man drink the Mickey Finn. They would then rob all his money, jewelry, and even the rich clothes he wore when he fell asleep. So they set up a little, temporary bar on the roadside. They put in a jar their last remaining liquor and combined it with some strong sleeping pills. The wealthy guy then came along on his way to the castle. One of the alcoholics named him, « Honorable sir, why don't you day continue with us, right? And the first one is at home! » Then he poured out a bottle of deceptive liquor. Yet the being of the Enlightenment drank no sort of alcohol. Nevertheless, he questioned why with their preferred medication these drunkards were so sweet. That was just not the way they were. He knew that it had to be some form of trick. And he'd wanted to teach them a lesson. He said, "It will be an embarrassment to be in an intoxicated condition before the monarch, or perhaps even the faint hint of liquor at my mouth. So please be so gracious as to wait for me here. I'll see you around when I return from the palace." As much as they liked they would not be willing to drink again. Yet they knew they needed to be careful and wait. The wealthy guy came back to the tiny street side bar later that day. The alcoholics have been eager to take a beer. They called him, and asked, "Honorable sir, why not appreciate the visit of your king? Take a sip of this fine liquor. Note, the first one is safe!" But the rich man just kept staring at the liquor bottle and bowl. He said, "I don't believe you. The bottle and glass of liquor are just like they were this morning. Unless it is like nice as you think it is, you'd have had plenty by yourself by now. Obviously, you couldn't help but consume it all! I'm no fool. You could have introduced some substance to the beer." Benares' wealthiest guy went on his way, and the drunkard group went back to their conspiring and shivering.

3.13 A Motherless Son (Betrayal)

King Brahmadatta once governed in northern India at Benares. He had a smart president, who was really happy with him. He named him Headman of a small frontier village to demonstrate his gratitude. His job was to serve the King and receive from the peasants the king's taxes.

Before long the villagers finally embraced the headman. Since the only King Brahmadatta had sent him, they have highly valued him. They came as often to support him as though he had been raised among them.

The headman was not only smart but also very arrogant. Collecting the king's taxes didn't give him an adequate incentive. He figured out a scheme to make himself wealthy after getting friends with a group of robbers.

The headman said to his mates, the thieves, "I'm trying to find loopholes and ways to bring all the villagers into the forest. It's going to be simple for me, because they consider me as one of their own. I'm going to hold them occupied in the woods, as you're entering the village and stealing everything of their money. Take all away until I have the citizen's home.

The headman gathered all the villagers as the day came, and guided them into the forest. The bandits have reached the vulnerable village according to schedule. They robbed everything they could think of interest. They killed all the defenseless cows in the area, and roasted and consumed the meat. The group gathered all of their stolen merchandise and fled at the end of the day.

It so happened that a traveling trader came to the village on the very same day to exchange his products. He had remained out of reach when he saw the robbers.

In the evening the headman took home all the villagers. He directed them to beat drums and create a lot of noise as they marched into the settlement. While the bandits were still there, they'd certainly noticed the villagers arriving.

People in the village noticed that they had been robbed, and all their cows had been dead and eaten in half. This has made them very unhappy. The traveling merchant appeared and said to them, 'Your faith in him has been compromised by this manipulative village headman. He must be a criminal bandit buddy. He just guided you home until they left with all of your valuables. Drums sound as strongly as practicable! This guy pretends to know nothing-as innocent as a newborn lamb! In reality, it is as though a son is doing something so disgusting that his mother will claim -'I'm not his mother. He isn't my family. My son is absolutely gone! "'News of the offense reached the king a short time ago, recalling the manipulative headman and executing him according to the statute.

3.14 Land Monks in the Leisure Garden of the King (Pupils without a Teacher)

Once upon a time, in the real country, there was a high-class wealthy guy who gave up his wealth and his simple existence. He went to the Woods of the Himalayas and stayed as a religious homeless man. He built his mind by practicing meditation, and acquired the highest awareness. He existed in strong mental conditions and shared tremendous inner peace and tranquility. He'd had 500 pupils before long.

In a year, as the rainy season was beginning, the pupils said to their instructor, "Hey wise lord, we'd like to go to the places where most people stay. We'd like to get some salt and other seasonings and carry them back here." The instructor replied, "You've got my permission. It'd be safe for you to do that, and come back when the rainy season is done.

The 500 pupils have gone to Benares and have begun staying in the royal pleasure garden. The following day they gathered alms in the villages outside the town gates. They did receive generous food gifts. They went within the town the next day. People were happy to give them food.

After a couple of days, people told the king, "My Lord King, 500 forest monks have come from the Himalayas to stay in your garden of enjoyment. They stay in a basic way, without luxuries. They regulate their senses and are considered to be

quite pleasant indeed." He knelt down, and showed reverence for him. He welcomed them to spend the whole four months of the rainy season living in the greenhouse. They agreed, and from that time on their food was provided in the palace of the King.

A similar holiday took place a short time ago. Drinking alcohol was enjoyed which the citizens felt would bring good luck. The King of Benares said, "Quality wine is generally not available to monks who actually stay in the woods. I must introduce them to others as a special gift." And he provided a huge quantity of the very finest quality wine to the 500 Forest monks.

The monks were not used to drink at all. They drank the wine of the king, and went back to the forest. They were totally wasted by the time they got there. Some of them started spinning and some started singing songs. Their bowls and other items are normally packed away neatly. Yet this time they just left it, here and there, lying there. They all quickly passed out for a drunken state.

We awakened after they had slept off their drunkenness, and realized the filthy state in which they had left it. They got emotional and said to each other, 'We've done a terrible thing that's not appropriate for holy men like US.' Their humiliation and guilt caused them to cry with remorse. They said, 'We've done this immoral stuff only because we're separated from our holy instructor.'

The 500 mountain monks abandoned the pleasure garden at the very moment, and headed to the Himalayas. Upon arrival they carefully packed away their bowls and other things, as

was their tradition. They then went to their beloved master, and politely accepted him.

He told them, are you my kids Mow? Have you found adequate food and lodgings in the town? Are you been satisfied, and united? "They answered. We were satisfied and together, Venerable Father. Yet we drank what we shouldn't have been eating. We missed much of our sense of common interest and self-control. We sang and yelled like crazy monkeys. It's good we didn't become monkeys! We drank champagne, we sang, we sang, and in the end we cried out of guilt. "The caring instructor said," Things like this will easily happen to pupils who have no instructor to lead them. Know therefore. Will not do anything like that in the future. "From that point on they lived together and rose in goodness.

3.15 The Religious One who wanted something Pure (Extremism)

The Enlightened Being had once existed in a society where most beliefs were very close. They learned that the way to alleviate emotional distress was then to let the body suffer. As odd as it is, most citizens believed that those who punished their bodies the most were the holiest of the saints! As all appeared to agree with this, the Bodhisatta wanted to find out whether that was valid with them.

He started functioning as an average normal citizen and according to the tradition of the times he became a holy man. This meant he gave up everything, including his shoes. He had left nude, his body still coated in ashes and soil.

And the flavor of healthy food does not ruin him; he allowed himself to consume only dirty stuff-garbage, dust, feces and cow dung.

Because he could focus without anyone interrupting him, he went to stay in the most hazardous area of the world. He backed backward like a shy animal because he had encountered a human being.

He lived his days beneath the woods in the wintertime and his nights out in the forest. And the cool water falling from the Heracles suspended from the roots of the tree saturated him in the afternoon. Then the dropping snow-shrouded him at night. He had his body experience the most intense cold in day and night in this way in winter.

He enjoyed his days outside in the summertime, and his evenings beneath the leaves. And, in the afternoon, the most intense rays of the sunburnt him. Then at night he'd been shielded from the last free air calming breezes. In this way he made his body feel the most intense temperatures every day and night in the season.

He suffered like that, seeking to get calm to his soul. He was so adamant he worked in this way throughout his life.

Instead, just before he was preparing to expire, he had a resurrected dream of himself in a land of fire. The dream hit him like lightning, and he realized immediately that all the forms he had abused his body were in vain! They hadn't given him peace of mind. Lo and behold, he died and was resurrected in a land of heaven, when he gave up his false convictions and kept on to the facts!

3.16 The Wisdom of Queen Tenderhearted (Lust)

The Enlightenment Being was once born into a rich, high-class family in Kasi, in northern India. He rose to youthful manhood and finished college. He then gave up ordinary wishes, and fled the realm of daily existence. He was a religious man, and went to the Himalayan woods to stay by himself. Over a long period he meditated, gained strong intellectual abilities, and was overflowing with inner peace. Having run out of the water, he came down to Benares town one day. He remained at the royal garden for the night. He cleaned himself in the morning, tied his twisted hair knot on top of his head and clothed in the fur of a black antelope. He rolled up the red bark robe which he usually carried. Then he went into town to get alms items. King Brahmadatta had been pacing back and forth on his terrace when he arrived at the palace entrance. He thought there was such a thing as absolute peace when he saw the modest-looking holy guy, this guy must have discovered it! "He took his staff to the house. The holy man relaxed on a comfortable sofa, and served the finest meal. He wished to thank the ruler. The king said, "You are welcome to stay forever in my royal garden. I must have the 'Four Necessities' - food, clothes, accommodation, and medication. By doing so, I can achieve dignity leading to redemption by a celestial realm." He lived the next 16 years staying in Benares royal forest. At that time, he learned all in the family of the king, and earned from the king the Four Needs.

One day King Brahmadatta determined that he would have to travel to a border region to set a rebellion down. Until leaving, he asked his wife to look after the holy man's needs. Its name was Tenderhearted Queen.

Every day she cooked food for the holy one. And one day he'd come late for his dinner. While waiting, Queen Tenderhearted was refreshing herself in a perfumed shower, clad in elegant clothes and jewelry, and lying down on the sofa.

The Awakening Being had in the meantime been meditating in an especially happy mental condition. He used the strength of his intellectual integrity to float through the air into the building, until he knew what time it was. When Queen Tenderhearted noticed his bark-robe rustling sound, she unexpectedly rose from her sofa. By doing so, her blouse unintentionally fell down for a second-so when he approached, the holy man glimpsed at her from the glass. He was taken aback by the rare sight of the great beauty of the queen.

Inside him grew to a passion, which had been suppressed but not destroyed. This looked much like a rise of a cobra, extending the head out of the bowl it is held in. His power has lost its pureness. Like a crow with a fractured leg he was injured.

The saintly guy was unwilling to consume his bread. He brought it back to his imperial garden temple house, and placed it under his pillow. His imagination was dominated by Queen Tenderhearted's definition of perfection. Her heart filled with love. For the next seven days he sat on his pillow, without eating or drinking.

The king wound up returning once again. He toured the area, and then went straight to see the holy man in the temple of the forest. He had thought he was ill when he noticed him lying in the hospital. He washed the room, and then stood alongside him. He began massaging his feet and said, "Reverend Sir, what's happened to you? Are you sick?" The holy man replied, "My great lord, my illness is that I'm trapped in chains of lust." "What do you want?" the Lord said. "My lord, Queen Tenderhearted." "Your honor," the king replied, "I will send you Tenderhearted. Come with me."

King Brahmadatta had his wife clad in her best garments and jewelry as they landed at the palace. Instead he asked her privately to help the poor, religious guy recover his innocence. She said. "I know what to do, my god, I'm going to help him." So the king gave her up and she fled the palace with the holy man. When they entered through the main gate she replied, "And it's dirty! Go back to the king to get a shovel and a bucket." He also had to paint fresh cow dung across the walls and floor! Then she told him to go to the castle, to get a bed for her. Next came a chair. She told him to get all these items one by one and he obediently obeyed. She sent him out to get water for her bath and a lot more. He went out to bathe her water and then made up the bed. We then settled down on the bed near each other. She abruptly caught him by the whiskers, rocked him back and forth, dragged him against her, asking, "Don't you know that you are a holy man and a priest?" Only then was he stunned by his insane infatuation and forced to understand who he is. Having recovered his self-awareness, he realized, "Ah what a pitiful condition I have sunk through. I have become overwhelmed by my urge to become a slut. Starting with just a woman's eyes, this insane ambition might take me into a devil's place. My body was burning, as though I had been fired in the heart with an arrow of lust. Upon having taken her back from the holy man he said to the king, "I no longer want your queen, but she was my only desire before I had her, but after I had her one desire led to the other endlessly and led only to hell." The wise Queen Tenderhearted gave the holy man a great gift, using her wisdom and her comprehension of life. Instead of profiting from his vulnerability, she returned his integrity.

The Enlightenment Being soared into the air in absolute harmony, prayed to the king and then fled effortlessly to the mountains of the Himalayas. He never returned to the ordinary world again. After meditating in peace and joy for many years, he died and was resurrected in a world of high heaven.

3.17 Two Ways Of Beating A Drum (Excess)

There was once a drummer living in a small country village. He learned that there would be a fair in the town of Benares. So he decided to go to play his drums and earn some income. He took his son with him to perform music composed for two sets of drums.

The two drummers, dad and wife, went to the Fair of Benares. They have been really effective. All loved playing their drums and gave them generously. At the conclusion of the fair, they continued their journey home to their small community.

They had to move through a deep forest on their journey. It was really risky because of the theft by the travelers.

The drummer boy tried to defend his dad and himself from muggers. And he pounded his drums vigorously, without slowing. "More noise, the stronger!" said he. The drummer took away his wife. He explained to him that when large groups, particularly royal processions, had passed by, they used to beat drums. They did so daily, in a very dignified way, as if they were not afraid of anyone. They will beat a roll of drums, stay quiet, beat again, and so forth. He told his son to do the same to trick the Muggers into believing that there was a mighty lord passing by.

But the boy ignored the advice of his aunt. He thought he knew best. He thought he might know best. "The more noise, the better!" he said.

Elsewhere, the boy is being drummed by a group of muggers. At first they thought it must be a powerful rich man with a high degree of security. Nevertheless, they heard the drumming go on in a wild way without stopping. They realized it sounded scary, like a terrified little dog barking at a big happy dog.

So they went to inquire and only found the dad and son. They beat them, stole all their money and fled into the wood.

3.18 A Mother's Wise Advice (Non-violence)

Brahmadatta's son once governed justly in Benares, in northern India. It happened that the King of Kosala battled, killed the King of Benares, and rendered the Daughter his own queen.

During the end, the Queen's son fled into the sewers, slipping backward. He gradually created a major army in the countryside and surrounded the area. He sent a letter to the king, his father's murderer and his mother's uncle. He asked him to give up the kingdom or war a war.

This warning was noticed by her son by the prince's mother, the Queen of Benares. She was a sweet and loving lady who tried to escape abuse and pain and murder. She sent her son a letter-" It's not required the dangers of fighting. It will be better to close the entrance to the city. Eventually, the citizens would strip away the shortage of food, water and firewood, and offer the city to them without any fight. "The prince agreed to obey the wise advice of his mother. Seven days and nights his army blockaded the city. Then the citizens kidnapped their leader, cut off his head, and handed it over to the prince. He stormed the city victoriously and became Benares' new ruler.

3.19 A Lesson from a Snake (The Value of Goodness)

King Brahmadatta of Benares once had a rather good priest as a counselor. He hailed from a powerful house of nobility. He was clever and full of experience. In his wealth and intelligence, he was kind, keeping nothing back. People considered him a loving and good guy.

He conditioned his mind to stop five harmful acts by completing the five training courses. He found that giving up some negative behavior made him happier on his own: killing life, since you had to hurt someone else in order to punish somebody yourself. Taking what isn't offered, because that makes the owner upset at you. Doing wrong physically, adds to resentment and envy. Knowing how he had worked, King Brahmadatta said, "He is a real decent guy." The priest was surprised as he knew something about the meaning of goodness. Yet I wonder what he actually likes most about me. Is it my ethnicity, my noble birth or the riches of my family? Was this my wonderful schooling and comprehensive knowledge? What is that for my goodness? I have to find the reason for that.' So, in order to satisfy his query, he wanted to perform the experiment. He should claim to be a thief! On the following day as he entered the house, he went by the royal coin manufacturer. He had marked out gold coins. The good priest, not wanting it to be held in his position, took a coin and walked out of the palace. Finally, on the third day a whole bunch of gold coins was caught by the king's favored priest. The moneymaker this time didn't worry about the status or prestige of the priest. He yelled, "This is the third instance, the king's dignity has been stolen by you." Hanging on him he yelled, "I trapped the thief that robes the King! I caught a thief who robes the King! I caught the theft of the State!" Unexpectedly, a crowd came rushing in, shouting, "Aah! You tried to be greater than us! An indication of goodness!"

But they managed to pass past a few snake charmers on their journey. Any of the men from the king's court were amused with a poisonous cobra. They caught him by the tail and by the collar and enveloped him to show him how brave they were.

The prisoner tied up said, "Take caution, please, not taking the cobra by the ear. Do not pick it by the ears. And don't cover the dangerous snake around your ankles. Maybe he will bite you and put your life to an abrupt end!" The snake charmers said, "You stupid priest, you don't get this cobra. He's well-mannered and honestly really sweet. He's not evil like you! You're a robber who's robbed from the king. Because of your wickedness and dishonest conduct, you're getting taken away with your hands bound behind your back. But there's no reason to bind up a nice snake!" "They responded, 'This is the robber who took the royal treasury from you.' The king said. "Then

---

discipline him according to the rules." The priest's counselor said, "My lord father, I am no thief! "Why did you carry gold coins out of the palace then?" the King questioned.

The priest explained, "I've just done this as an idea to check whether you value me and appreciate me better than anyone. Is it because of my family heritage and riches, or because of my excellent knowledge? Because of those items, I've been able to get away with taking one or two gold coins. Or do you most of all appreciate my goodness? It's obvious that by getting a couple of coins I no longer have the name 'goo'. "Even a poisonous cobra, which does not hurt anybody, is named 'healthy.' There is no need for any other word!" To illustrate the lesson he had learnt, the wise priest recited: "High birth and riches and even vast intelligence, I think, are less valued than goodness is, by humanity."

He requested permission to abandon the service of the King in the ordinary world to become a monk of the wood. Upon multiple refusals. In the end, the king gave his permission.

The priest went to the Himalayas, and quietly meditated. When he died he was raised anew in a kingdom with heaven.

3.20 The Careless Lion (Circumspection)

The five preparation phases were not yet established in the world for some time. Benares was home to a very rich man who kept a huge herd of cattle. He employed a guy to take charge of these.

The herdsman brought the cattle to the forest for pasture at the time of year when the rice paddies were lined with the green rising rice plants. From there he took the meat, butter and cheese to the Benares rich man.

That just happened. The cattle in such a risky condition are in the wood. A meat-eating lion had been residing nearby. Sensing the lion's presence has held the bovine in persistent terror. Which made the cows nervous and high-strung, making them too frail to give more than a limited amount of milk?

One day the cattle owner told the herdsman why he carried only a limited amount of milk and butter, and cheese. He responded, "Sir, the cows need to be relaxed and happy to give a lot of milk. Your cows are still afraid and nervous because of a nearby lion. So they don't offer much milk."

"I see ……" the wealthy man said. Thinking like an animal trapper, he said, "Is the lion strongly related to some other species?" The herdsman answered, "Sir, there happens to be a number of deer live in the forest. They're named 'minideer' because they're so small. Even the adults-only grow to be about one foot tall. The lion has been really popular with a certain minideer doe." Benares' rich man said, "That's why my adults only grow to be about one foot tall." The herdsman has pursued precisely the instructions of his manager. He was so overjoyed when the lion saw his beloved minideer doe, that he cast all caution into the sea. Before really sniffing the air surrounding her, he quickly began to lap her up all over excitedly. He slipped into the venomous pit because of so much excitement and not enough restraint. The unfortunate lion died at the scene.